THE HOLOCAUST

SURVIVAL AND RESISTANCE

Patricia Levy

RAINTREE
Steck-Vaughn
PUBLISHERS

A Harcourt Company

Austin   New York
www.raintreesteckvaughn.com

Titles in the series: Causes • The Death Camps •
Survival and Resistance • After the Holocaust

Published by Raintree Steck-Vaughn Publishers,
an imprint of Steck-Vaughn Company

Library of Congress Cataloging-in-Publication Data

Levy, Patricia, 1951-
  Survival and resistance / Patricia Levy.
  p. cm. -- (Holocaust)
  ISBN 0-7398-3260-3
  1. Holocaust, Jewish (1939–1945)--Juvenile literature. 2. War crime
trials--Juvenile literature. 3. Holocaust, Jewish (1939-1945)--Moral and
ethical aspects--Juvenile literature. 4. World war, 1939-1945--Jews--
Rescue--Juvenile literature. [1. Holocaust, Jewish (1939-1945) 2.
World War, 1939-1945--Jewsih resistance. 3. Holocaust survivors.] I.
Title. II. Holocaust (Austin, Tex.)

  D804.34 .L5 2001
  943.53'18--dc21   00-066501

Printed in Italy. Bound in the United States.
1 2 3 4 5 6 7 8 9 0 06 05 04 03 02

*Cover photo: (Wiener Library)
Jews are taken from the
Warsaw Ghetto to one of the
many concentration camps in
Poland.*

*Page 1: (Wiener Library) The
Vilnius partisans return to the
ghetto after liberation in July
1944.*

Acknowledgments

AKG 4, 8, 11, 12, 14, 17, 21,
27, 33, 38, 42, 50, 55, 56;
Archive Photos 15; Camera Press
19, 23, 24, 25, 30, 31, 36, 45,
53, 54, 57; Hulton Getty 22, 35;
Impact Picture Library 59;
Novosti Photo Library 41, 51,
52; Popperfoto 16; Jeremy
Schonfeld 13, 34; Wayland
Picture Library 47, 58; United
States Holocaust Memorial
Museum 10, 18, 20, 26, 28, 32,
39, 40, 43, 44, 48; Wiener
Picture Library 5, 6 (left), 6
(right), 7, 9, 29, 49.

CONTENTS

WHAT IS RESISTANCE?

By LATE 1941, World War II was in its third year, and Hitler's plan to exterminate the Jews of Europe was taking shape. Jews from all over the continent were being transported to concentration camps and sealed ghettos. If they didn't die on their way to the camps, most would be gassed or worked to death. Many were not transported to the camps at all. Instead, special mobile units of soldiers, called *Einsatzgruppen* killed large numbers of Jews in their villages and homelands. The *Einsatzgruppen* were particularly active in Poland, Ukraine, and the Soviet Union. In all, as many Jews were massacred by the *Einsatzgruppen* as were killed in the camps. For all but a handful of Jews, emigration and refuge in a foreign country was not an option.

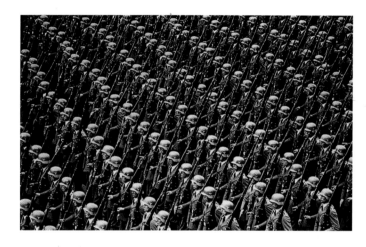

Above: Nazi soldiers march in Nuremberg, Germany, in 1937.

Left: This map of Europe shows some of the places where rebellions or other acts of Jewish resistance took place.

The Ultimate Sacrifice

Samuel Pisar lived in the Bialystok ghetto in Poland. In 1943, as the Germans liquidated the ghetto, he hid with 30 others in a cellar:

...my teacher...Professor Bergman was rocking his infant son, trying to stop his coughing. On the other side of the trapdoor above us came the shouts of German search parties and the barking of their dogs.

We all fell silent; only the baby's coughing

continued ... A man crawled over and put his hand over the baby's mouth. The coughing ceased. Minutes passed. The child sank limply to the ground.

All the while Professor Bergman sat petrified. I knew he was not a coward. Even then, I understood that if he could think or feel anything at all, he was weighing one life against thirty, even if that life was his own son's.

(Quoted in Martin Gilbert, *The Holocaust: The Jewish Tragedy*)

For most Jews, all they could do was try to survive. For some, this took the form of resistance.

Entire nations, armed with all the machinery of war, buckled under the German onslaught. It is therefore all the more remarkable that under such terrible circumstances individuals fought back.

During these years, Jews hid, escaped, and bribed their way out of Germany. Many worked in the labor and death camps and in ghettos. They wrote down what they had witnessed, kept secret radios, published pamphlets and documents, held secret religious services, helped other Jews to escape, stole food, and brought comfort to their families and friends. Citizens of many nations—Poles, Germans, French, Italians, Bulgarians, and Dutch—individually sheltered Jews at great risk to their own lives and those of their families. Many occupied states prevented the deportation of their Jews. All of the people and countries that helped the Jews could be said to have resisted the Holocaust.

Below: Jews from Bialystok being marched away— probably to the Auschwitz death camp

Armed Resistance

It has been estimated that 1.5 million Jews took part in armed resistance against the Germans, many of them dying in the process and provoking massive reprisals against their families and communities. Jews fought in the French resistance movement, among Polish and Soviet resistance groups in the woods of Poland, Belarus, and Ukraine, and in the ghettos and the death camps. There was even a Jewish resistance group, the *Baumgruppe*, that operated in Berlin, Germany, until 1942.

Those Jews who chose to fight faced terrible adversity. Many of them fought after months or even years on starvation rations, grueling forced labor, and many more years of rejection and hatred by the state to which they had been loyal. They had few weapons and no support from the Allied forces. Some faced anti-Semitism from those who, like them, were considered enemies of Germany but were scared of reprisal. Most of those who fought against the German regime knew that if they were discovered helping Jews they would suffer at best immediate death and at worst days of torture when they might be forced to betray their comrades. They knew that terrible reprisals would be made not just against their families but against their whole community.

Below: Werner Steinbrink and Edith Fraenkel were members of the Baumgruppe, a group of young Communists who operated in Berlin until May 1942 when they were captured and shot. They organized anti-Nazi poster campaigns and destroyed an anti-Soviet exhibition in Berlin.

Worse still than all of these things was the overwhelming superiority of those that they fought. Very often the Jews' best hope was not that they could defeat their enemies but that their deaths might frustrate their enemies' aims or cause temporary inconvenience.

Below: The Vilnius ghetto community organized theatrical and musical performances such as this one.

The Vilnius Ghetto 1943

The dilemma of those Jews who wished to fight the Nazis can be seen in the events surrounding one breakout from the ghetto of Vilnius in Lithuania in 1943. A group of young people obtained some weapons and joined a partisan group in the Narotch forest nearby. They engaged the Germans in battle just outside the city; several of them were captured. When the Germans learned that they were Jewish escapees, every member of their families and the leaders of all the work parties that they came from were shot. Afterward the entire ghetto was divided into work parties of 10. If one person disappeared, the rest of their work party would die. The Vilnius ghetto newspaper called those who had run away to fight "traitors to the Jewish people" and said that the proper thing for those in the ghetto to do was to stay in it and not risk the lives of the 20,000 other Jews who could not escape.

Dying as an Act of Resistance

There were many ways to resist the Nazi goal of the annihilation of the Jews instead of fighting, running away, or surviving. Part of the German strategy with the Jews was to make them feel less than human. In the camps people were tattooed with numbers, given inadequate uniforms, underfed, and had their possessions taken and their hair cut off. Primo Levi, an Italian Jew who survived Auschwitz, wrote about this drive to dehumanize the Jews. Levi saw the challenge to maintain a sense of self as a way of resisting and thwarting Nazis. Everyone who maintained a sense of their own identity in the face of some of the most horrific things that one human being could do to another was resisting the Holocaust, even if he or she died in the death camps.

Below: One way of humiliating the Jews was to force them to wear an identifying yellow star of David. Some Jews wore it with shame while others wore it proudly.

Some people even chose death when they might have survived. A survivor, Szymon Datner, recalls one man, a wheelmaker, who was being taken to the camps with his family and was urged by his wife to run away—which he could easily have done. But he refused to leave his family and went to the Treblinka death camp with them. Other stories tell of adults volunteering to go to the gas chambers with orphaned children, and nurses accompanying their patients to the camps when they might have stayed behind.

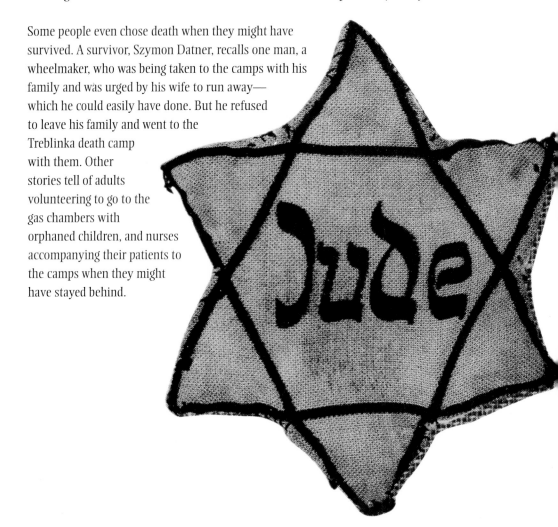

Left: Shmuel Zygielbojm lived in Warsaw with his wife and family until 1939. A socialist member of the Jewish Council, he advocated passive resistance to the forced movement of Warsaw's Jews into a ghetto area.

Shmuel Zygielbojm

Shmuel Zygielbojm was a Polish Jew from Warsaw who was sent to London in 1940 to represent the interests of the Polish Jews in London. He became a leading speaker and made the fate of the Jews known to as many people in London as would listen. In 1943, after the Warsaw ghetto uprising, he committed suicide in London. His suicide note explained that he had not been fortunate enough to die with his comrades in Warsaw with weapons in their hands. He had felt he could no longer live while the Jewish people were being annihilated. His letter concluded "By my death I wish to express my vigorous protest against the apathy with which the world regards and resigns itself to the slaughter of the Jewish people."

SURVIVING THE HOLOCAUST

Escape and Hiding

B Y 1933 many Jews in Germany and Poland chose to leave for places that they hoped would be safer—Austria, France, Holland, and Belgium. As Hitler's plans for the Jews became clearer, by 1939, 300,000 people—30 percent of the Jewish population of Germany—had left their country. In Poland, about 400,000 Jews had emigrated by 1939.

After 1939, as Germany invaded and occupied more countries, the number of Jews living in German-occupied territories swelled by two million. Two years later, with the invasion of Russia, three million more came under German control. Escape was impossible for such huge numbers, and those remaining in Germany were either shipped into Poland to live in the ghettos or found some way to live within Germany. Many pretended to be Gentiles (non-Jews); some were hidden by kind neighbors or by people who took money to hide them. Some were posed as *Mischling* (half Jews, or those married to Germans). Even for the estimated 5,000 Jews who lived in hiding in Berlin, life carried a

Below: This wedding photo of a Jewish couple, Herman de Leeuw and Annie Pais, was taken in Amsterdam in 1942. Only one of the people in the photograph, Samual Schrivjer (sixth from the left), survived the war.

Life in Hiding

With the help of Gentile friends, Bronisawa Goldfischer survived the war. The events she describes here took place when she was 13 years old and living in Lwow, Poland.

In December 1942 it was obvious that sooner or later all the Jews in the ghetto would be eliminated. In the face of this my father decided to save at least me, found a place for me with a Polish family whom he paid 15,000 zlotys.... Despite the danger they were in because of me—they risked their own lives by taking me in—they looked after me like I was one of their own children, and it was thanks to them that I survived.

[One day an intelligence agent came to Bronisawa's house] ... he said I was very good at playing the part of an Aryan girl. Then he searched the wardrobe and to his surprise he found a photograph of me in a special dress kneeling down to take Communion. My parents had had that photograph taken in the ghetto by a photographer they knew... This obviously misled the agent because he asked me a few more questions about my papers and left.

(Quoted in Maria Hochberg-Mariañska and Noe Grüss, *The Children Accuse*)

---

constant threat of discovery or betrayal by their neighbors once their money had run out. It is thought that 200,000 Jews survived in hiding in German-occupied territories.

After 1939, small numbers of European Jews continued to escape across Europe to the unoccupied region of France, which was self-governing. From there, about 12,000 were brought into Portugal or by sea to Casablanca, Morocco. Some 20,000 found their way to Shanghai in China while 4,000 escaped to Kobe in Japan. About 13,000 German Jews with enough capital to prove they would not be a burden on their new home were able to get visas for Great Britain or Palestine. Until the invasion of the Soviet Union, the Nazis were still willing to allow emigration at a price.

Below: In 1936 these Parisian Jews lived peaceful lives within French society. This was soon to change.

Betrayal and Rescue

It was German policy from the 1930s onwards to 'Aryanize' Jewish property. By that they meant confiscate it and give it to German citizens – and later – citizens of German occupied territories such as France and Poland. This gave an incentive to ordinary people – neighbours and friends of the Jews, to betray them to the authorities. Anyone seen to be a friend of the Jews was a traitor and could suffer terribly. The Nazis perfected their incentives to encourage betrayal of the Jews: they persuaded people to give Jews up by saying that they might get the house of the person they betrayed. The alternative was, if they helped them, to go to the gas chambers with them.

On the other hand vast numbers of people, for many different reasons, risked their lives to help the Jews: anti-Semitic Polish nationalists because they wished to stop the Nazis grow in

Below: Like millions of other Jews, the survival of this man and child depended on the sympathy of strangers, chance or their own limited ability to protect themselves.

Rabbi Solomon Schonfeld

As early as 1933 the young and charismatic Rabbi Schonfeld could see that the Jews of Europe were in terrible danger. He lived and looked after a congregation in North London and had access to Jewish families that would take in Jewish refugees, especially children. At that time Britain would only allow in a small number of Jews, and only on the guarantee that a British person would provide for them. From the mid-1930s he began bringing groups of refugees into Britain, using his friends and congregation as guarantors. They were housed at first in his own house, in the school he had established, and later in refugee hostels. One of his brothers tells the story of how on his return home from university he found a child asleep in his bed with another sleeping under it! The war brought an end to his efforts, as it meant that refugees couldn't travel to Britain, and he spent the war years caring for the children that he had brought over. After the war he travelled around Poland, looking for orphan children. It is estimated that Rabbi Schonfeld rescued about 3,500 Jews, mostly children.

power; Christians because they believed the Nazis' actions were wrong and unChristian; neighbours and strangers in exchange for cash or out of pity. In Chambon-sur-Lignon in France, the entire town formed an underground transport system to smuggle Jews to safety. In Holland there was a two-day general strike in opposition to Nazi policies towards the Jews, which ended in terrible punishments for those involved. Towards the end of the war many people, apathetic or too scared to help during the Holocaust, suddenly realized that sheltering a few Jews might help them at the end of the war, when they might be called to account for their lack of action.

Right: Solomon Schonfeld with some of the children he rescued.

The Frank Family

Otto Frank and his family were German Jews who left Germany in 1933 when the Nazi rise to power began. They lived openly in Amsterdam in the Netherlands through the German invasion and the imposition of anti-Jewish laws, until 1942 when transportations of Jews to the death and concentration camps began. They went into hiding in a secret annex above Otto's business premises. They planned their period of hiding in advance and made all the necessary arrangements for money and help. They chose not to leave Amsterdam for a "safe" country and remained together as a family, despite the terrible dangers.

For two years, Otto, his wife, and two daughters, Anne and Margot, lived in hiding with another Jewish family, the van Pelses (called the van Daans in the diary Anne kept) and a family friend, Fritz Pfeffer (called Albert Dussel in the diary). They had to remain completely hidden at all times, being careful that they

Below: Jewish women arrive at Auschwitz in 1944. Anne Frank, her mother, and her sister would also have gone through the process of having their hair shaved off.

Anne Frank's Diary

Shut up inside the attic, Anne's only contacts with the outside world were the people that her family relied on to bring them food. Her diary entries are about quarrels, her growing love for Peter van Pels, and, occasionally, anti-Semitism and the war. Here she writes about her sadness:

I wander from one room to another, downstairs and up again, feeling like a song bird whose wings have been brutally clipped and who is beating itself in utter darkness against the bars on its cage. "Go outside, laugh, take a breath of fresh air," a voice cries within me, but I don't even feel a response any more; I go and lie on the divan and sleep, to make the time pass more quickly, and the stillness and the terrible fear, because there is no way of killing them.

Below: An excellent student, Anne Frank—seen here at age 11—dreamed of becoming a writer.

made no noises that might arouse suspicions. The youngest daughter, Anne, endured the 25 months of hiding by writing a diary addressed to an imaginary friend, Kitty. (The diary was published after the war as *The Diary of a Young Girl*.) She developed a relationship with Peter van Pels, who was two years older than her. Strains emerged between the two families in the difficult conditions they were forced to live in. They had a radio and heard news of what was going on in the war. Anne even listened to a British broadcast describing the gas chambers. Otto's employees and friends risked their own lives to bring the Franks food. Finally the Franks were discovered, or perhaps betrayed. They spent a few weeks in Westerbork transit camp in Holland and were then transported to Auschwitz, where Mrs. Frank and Mrs. van Pels died. Anne and Margot were transferred to Bergen-Belsen, where they both died of typhoid.

Surviving in the Ghettos

The ghettos of Poland and occupied Russia were created as a short-term way of containing the millions of Jews until they could be shipped to slave labor or death camps. The most run-down, unsanitary sections of the larger cities were walled off, and all Jews were given a few days to find accommodation within these ghetto areas. At first the ghettos were open, but by 1942 most were sealed off from the rest of the city. Telephones and radios were removed, parks and open spaces were all outside the walls, there was little or no sanitation or running water, and the inhabitants were kept too tired, hungry, and crowded to maintain minimum standards of hygiene and cleanliness. Fuel was scarce, and rations consisted of about 1,100 calories per person at best, often consisting of spoiled food rejected by the outside community—largely sour bread, turnips, and potatoes. (Two thousand calories a day is generally considered the minimum to maintain human health.) Most families were lucky to have a single room to themselves.

Those who had managed to smuggle valuables into the ghetto fared better. In many ghettos they were able to buy exemption from forced labor while their funds lasted, and they could buy smuggled or black market food.

Below: Between 1939 and 1945, people did many desperate things in order to survive. Here wealthy Poles are cutting up a dead horse in order to survive a siege in Warsaw.

Left: Abandoned Jewish children beg in the streets of the Warsaw ghetto in 1941.

Orphans in the Ghetto

The increase in numbers of orphans in the ghettos was horrific. By November 1941 there were 10,000 orphaned children living in the Warsaw ghetto. About 2,000 of them lived in orphanages set up by the Jewish Councils. The other 8,000 lived on the street. By 1942, 25,000 children were in institutions within the ghetto, and 75,000 lived in the streets, where they formed gangs, begged, or found some way of making a living—selling cigarettes or candies, smuggling, or doing odd jobs. Survival for these children depended on luck and judgment. The children's centers set up by the Nazis were not safe places, since their objective was to keep the children together where they could be easily transported to the camps. One orphaned survivor was Zbyseck, a cigarette seller: "Everybody I was with died in 1941. I travel around, occasionally pinching something. The day before yesterday some kids set on me so I punched one on the nose till he cried and then I tripped the other one and he ran…. No one jokes with me."

(From Zieman Joseph, *The Cigarette Sellers of Three Crosses Square*. Quoted in Ruby Rohrlich (ed), *Resisting the Holocaust*)

People quickly began to die from hunger in the ghettos, about 11,000 in Warsaw in 1941 alone. They also began to die from typhus, heart disease, dysentery, tuberculosis, and gastroenteritis.

But people also learned how to survive, by making things to sell outside, opening cafes and shops inside, forging work permits, making clothes, boots—anything they could think of. Where there was soil, small plots of vegetables were grown. Smuggling quickly developed, with children often being the ones sent outside the ghettos to buy food on the black market, while the parents worked in the slave factories. People learned to hide from the squads that daily came into the ghetto looking for workers for forced labor. Early warning systems were set up, giving people time to hide or escape from the Nazis searching the buildings. There was a boom in marriages in the ghetto as people sought strength and comfort in the family unit. Religious and cultural organizations developed, people played instruments, sang, and put on plays in the evenings. Above all they cooperated with the Germans, since that represented their best chance of survival.

Below: A German soldier patrols the Cracow ghetto, looking for people to fill the transports to the death camps. People without the proper documents could be designated to be sent to the camps.

A Hanukkah Celebration in the Lodz Ghetto

Hunger, cold and conflicts were all forgotten. Shoemakers and tailors, physicians, lawyers and pharmacists, all at one, we were one big family. That could not have happened in Berlin... but here, behind the barbed wire, something existed that united us all—our Jewishness. When they sang together, they forgot their suffering and misery; they were still alive and in song they praised God, who many times before had performed miracles. When they sang about the little lamp whose oil for one day lasted eight, the singers regained their courage and their hope.

(Ruth Alton's testimony, Leo Baeck Institute Archives, quoted in Lucy Dawidowicz, *The War Against the Jews*)

The *Judenrat*

Very few Germans policed the ghettos. Inside the ghettos the *Judenrat*, or the Jewish Council, followed Nazi orders and ran the ghettos. For the most part the *Judenrat* and the Jewish police were just people pulled out of the crowd and forced on pain of death to do the work. They collected taxes, maintained files on addresses and numbers of Jews, and administered the rationing. They even provided a police force to select first the destitute and criminals, then the children, the sick and old, and then the exhausted skilled workers for transportation to the slave and death camps. The Jewish officials justified their actions by claiming that, by sending the required number of Jews to the transports, they were saving the lives of the others. Others simply did it to save their own families.

Below: These men in the Warsaw ghetto were lined up and searched some time in 1943, during the violent ghetto uprising of that year.

Surviving in the Forests

Thousands of Jews fleeing from the sudden, massive German advance into the Baltic states in June 1941 found refuge in the forests on the borders of Poland, Belarus, Lithuania, and Ukraine. They were joined by hundreds of Russian soldiers escaping from advancing Germans, as well as civilians unwilling to be shipped to Germany to work as slaves in the factories. Besides taking part in guerrilla attacks, the Jewish resistance groups that formed here also sheltered the many Jews who were scattered and helpless in the woods. One group in particular, the Bielski Otriad, took in every Jewish person whom they found wandering in the woods. Jews were lucky to find the group. Polish and Russian partisan groups were just as likely to murder them for their possessions. The Bielski group numbered several thousand. Its members lived in a settlement deep in the Nolibocka forest, where they set up a gun repair shop, meat processing factory, and boot factory. Craftsmen used the materials they found in the forests to supply most of their needs. At first they raided local farms for food, but they were soon trading repaired and stolen guns with other partisan groups for food. A very primitive social system emerged—with those who had been businessmen in Berlin or Warsaw almost useless to the group, while simple peasant

Below: The Bielski Otriad was a Jewish partisan group that operated successfully until liberation by Russian troops. Simple peasants, the Bielski brothers knew how to survive in the forests and were responsible for the rescue of more than 1,000 Jews.

farmers like the Bielski brothers organized and ruled the community. Of the intellectuals and professionals who made it into the woods, only doctors, dentists, and nurses were of any use to the group. Despite this, everyone was given rations. In this way, former city dwellers who had no hope of surviving alone in the forest made it to the end of the war.

Above: Many other partisan groups operated in the same forest as the Bielski group, but few of them tolerated Jews.

Children in the Forests

Many people were never fortunate enough to find a group like the Bielski Otriad. In March 1943, a 12-year-old boy named Matti Drobless escaped from the Warsaw ghetto with his older sister and younger brother:

Our survival was based on our will to live and the talents we adopted. We stole food from the farms and removed articles of clothing from the washlines. We scrounged and when there was no alternative we sent our youngest brother into homes to beg. We taught him prayers and instructed him to pose as a Polish war orphan…

…We never met another Jew in our wanderings through the forests.

(Quoted in Martin Gilbert, *The Holocaust: The Jewish Tragedy*)

Surviving the Camps

By October 1941 mass deportations of Jews to specially built death camps in Poland had begun. Some of these camps, such as Auschwitz, also contained factories and mines where slave labor was used. On arrival at the camps as many as 80 percent of the Jews from the transports were immediately murdered. Others survived— doctors, nurses, dentists, and technicians were useful in running the camp, and musicians were often sent to the camp orchestra. Others were able to survive in indoor assignments such as the factories. But much of the work consisted of hard manual labor: mining, building, and quarrying. Most people quickly perished from exposure to the harsh Polish winter, malnourishment, disease, and exhaustion.

A "privileged" position for a prisoner was as a *Sonderkommando* —a male selected to work in the gas chambers sorting through dead bodies and discarded clothes. *Sonderkommandos* received extra rations and good clothes. But they knew that they would die, since their first task on being selected was to take the previous *Sonderkommandos* to the gas chambers. Others, usually criminals, were made into kapos, people who supervised the work of the slave laborers. They had many privileges in return for their brutal treatment of the other inmates.

Below: Auschwitz death camp and its satellite camps remain as a testimony to the countless people who died there.

Mengele's Experiments

Some people survived because they were selected for medical experimentation—although thousands more died horrific deaths as a result of the experiments of men like Dr. Josef Mengele, a Nazi physician at Auschwitz. One of the few ways for Jewish children to survive the initial selections was by being chosen for Mengele's experiments. Ernest Spiegel and his twin sister were chosen for the experiments. He was put in charge of a barracks of twin boys. In 1944 there were about 200 of them still alive, relatively well looked after and waiting to be chosen for experimentation. On a visit in October of that year by a high-ranking Nazi, the children were nearly sent to the gas chambers but were spared when Mengele intervened. When Auschwitz was evacuated in 1945, 33 sets of twins had survived.

Illness saved some people. Minor illnesses were treated in the camp hospitals, and in them the sick had a chance to recover a little strength. This was a risky business though, because patients ran the constant risk of being selected for the gas chambers. When Poland was liberated, those in Auschwitz who were too sick to be included in the death marches westward (the Germans' attempts to escape from the advancing Allies) were abandoned in the camp and were found by the Russian troops.

Above: Eva and Miriam Moses were selected to take part in the experiments of Dr. Mengele and thus survived their years in Auschwitz while most of their family perished.

Just as important as physical survival was psychological survival. Most people lost their families in the selections and gave up in despair. Others were able to form new relationships within their work parties and found support in that way. Some were inspired by their religion, while for others the determination to survive kept them going.

Surviving the Death Marches

By January 1945 German troops were in retreat across Russia and much of Eastern Europe, and the death camps of Poland were threatened with liberation. Rather than have the evidence of the previous five years fall into Allied hands, the Germans evacuated the death camps, and vast numbers of malnourished people were forced to walk hundreds of miles into German territory. The marches were chaotic. No preparations were made for transporting such huge numbers of people. Stragglers were shot. The marches took place in the dead of winter; surviving them must have taken an amazing act of will. At the end of the marches, thousands were crammed into camps that were horrifically overcrowded, even by German standards of camp life. Typhoid epidemics broke out, people starved to death, and there was even evidence of cannibalism among the desperate inmates.

Ironically, death came to many of the German concentration camp inmates after liberation. Allied soldiers, stunned by what they encountered, offered oatmeal, sugar, salt, dried milk powder, and canned meat—food that was too rich for the starving inmates. Typhoid carried off others. At Bergen-Belsen, 300 people died each day after liberation.

Right: American soldiers liberate Dachau concentration camp in April 1945.

Below: Thousands of starving Jews were herded to Bergen-Belsen at the end of the death marches. Anne Frank and her sister Margot died of typhoid in the camp. This picture shows conditions after liberation in 1945.

The Luck of Sim Kessel

Sim Kessel was a French boxer who was caught smuggling arms for the French resistance. He eventually found himself working in the mines at Jaworzno, a satellite camp of Auschwitz in Poland. His chances of surviving such work were small, and he was eventually selected to go to the gas chambers. Standing naked with the other emaciated men in the snow, waiting to be marched off to his death, he noticed that one of the SS men had a broken nose and scars across his eyes, typical signs of an ex-boxer. Kessel walked up to him and said one word in German: "boxer". The guard saw Kessel's own boxing scars and asked him about his matches. Suddenly he ordered Kessel, still naked, to get on his motorcycle. Kessel obeyed and the guard took him to the hospital. Later, on a death march, Kessel was put in an open freight car and made to lie down for five days, tangled up with 70 other men. When the two men beside him died, Kessel took their blankets and burrowed beneath their corpses to keep out the biting winter winds. Only 9 people of the 70 in his freight car survived.

RESCUE FROM HOME AND ABROAD

The Fate of the Jews in the Occupied States of Europe

AUSTRIA AND Czechoslovakia conformed to German policy almost as soon as they were invaded and initiated anti-Jewish legislation and controls over Jewish activities and life. By the end of the war, all the surviving Jews were either *Mischling* (of mixed Jewish ancestry) or had survived in hiding. In France the pro-Nazi Vichy government deported all Jewish refugees to the death camps, and later even French Jews were deported. Belgium and Holland also deported Jews from within their borders. Romania probably had the worst record of murder, enacting its own anti-Jewish legislation long before German troops reached it, carrying out pogroms (mass murder) and deportations. In Yugoslavia and Greece most of the Jewish population perished. Hungary took in many refugees from Germany, Czechoslovakia, and Poland, and although there were deportations and pogroms, most Jews remained relatively safe until Hungary was invaded in 1943. Deportations then began on a massive scale.

Below: Jewish deportees arriving at the Theresienstadt ghetto in Czechoslovakia. Thirty thousand Jews from Berlin, Vienna, and Prague died there, and many more were deported to the death camps from there.

Left: These German Jews are being deported from Würzburg in Germany, probably to the Lublin ghetto in Poland.

Despite this tragic record, many countries tried to help the Jews. Luxembourg enabled many Jews to escape as far as France and Portugal. To its credit, Italy, a fascist state, was reluctant to deport Jewish residents and refugees. No Italian Jews were deported until 1943, when Germany invaded Italy. By that time many Jews had been helped to leave or had gone into hiding. In Bulgaria, one of Germany's allies, Jews were at first subject to anti-Semitic laws, and 11,000 were deported to Poland, but after public protests no more deportations were made. In Norway the Norwegian resistance helped about half the Jewish population escape into Sweden. In Denmark almost all of Denmark's 8,000 Jews were ferried to Sweden. Finland also refused to deport its population of 2,000 Jews.

The Spanish Blue Division

Between 1941 and 1943 a division of 40,000 volunteer Spanish soldiers served on the Russian front within the German army. But the Spaniards did not share the Nazi view of Jews, Slavs, and Russians as *Untermenschen* (members of an inferior race) and treated all people that they encountered with respect. The Spanish troops never actually opposed German treatment of Jews in the towns in which they were based, but they did not help carry out German policy. In the Spanish military hospitals, Jews and Slavs received treatment, and Jewish nurses and orderlies were protected from the constant selection of Jews for transport to the death camps. Spanish protection was short-lived, though. When the Spanish troops were withdrawn in 1943, all the Jews they had been protecting went back to the ghettos.

Individual Acts of Heroism

Although millions of people turned their backs on Jewish suffering, thousands of individuals risked their lives to help, some of whom came from very unusual backgrounds. One unexpected source of help for fleeing Jews came from a Polish thief. When the Lvov ghetto was being emptied and its Jews sent to death camps in June 1943, several people escaped into the sewers, where they had no way of surviving. While they were lost they encountered Leopold Socha, who used the sewers for smuggling. He took them to a dry hiding place in the sewers and brought food every day. Each week he brought clean clothes. Of the 21 people who Socha hid, 10 survived a year in the sewers and emerged when Poland was liberated. According to one of the people whom he had helped, a young Jewish woman named Halina Wind, Socha was hated by his neighbors for helping the Jews.

Left: Jewish partisan groups survived in the forests around Poland, Belarus, and Lithuania. Few of them survived the war. This group consists of refugees from Kaunas in Lithuania and operated around the Rudninkai forest near Vilnius.

God's Underground

When foreign Jews were interned in France after the German invasion, large numbers of Christian women (most men had been sent to war) went into the camps in order to help alleviate the conditions the Jews were living in. They provided healthcare and better food. Many of these women became elements in the "God's Underground" movement to evacuate the Jews from the camps. Children particularly were freed from the camps and found homes with Gentile families. Adults were also secretly evacuated and remained hidden for the duration of the war.

A Latvian farm worker, Yanis Lipke, regularly rescued Jews from the Riga ghetto and hid them in barns and chicken sheds belonging to his friends. In 1943 the Minsk ghetto was liquidated, and a few people hid in an underground bunker. They slowly began to starve to death, until one of them set out to find food. She met Anna Dvach, who gave her food and continued to keep the 13 Jews fed for six months until the arrival of Russian troops.

Above: Father Marie Benoit, a monk from Marseilles, worked with the French Resistance to smuggle thousands of Jewish children out of France and into Switzerland.

In Italy in 1943, Father Marie Benoit, a French priest, with the help of the Swiss, Hungarian, Romanian, and French embassies — as well as the Rome Chief of Police—helped Jews escape the round-up by issuing false identity papers. In 1944 an Italian policeman was sent to Dachau and murdered for helping 500 Jews get false papers and escape. In 1944, when the Kaunas ghetto was liquidated, a Lithuanian carpenter named Jan Pauvlavicus built a secret hiding place in his cellar and took in about 12 Jews, whom he protected for three weeks until liberation. After the war he was murdered by fellow Lithuanians for helping Jews. In France, Evelyne Sullerot hid 11 Jews among the mental patients that she looked after for the duration of the war. These are just a few instances of the phenomenal acts of heroism carried out during the Holocaust.

Oskar Schindler

A German businessman, Oskar Schindler found the war a useful way of making money, dealing on the black market and running an enamelware and munitions factory in Cracow. He employed only Jews and deliberately began making shell cases in order to have his factory designated vital to the war effort. When the Cracow ghetto was cleared, he built special barracks for his workers close to his factory. He personally paid for his workers' food, and on several occasions rescued them from the transports or, in one case, hanging, risking his own survival to do so. He spent huge amounts of the factory's profits on bribing officials to keep his factory running and his Jewish workers safe.

Left: Oskar Schindler was recognized by Israel as a righteous (virtuous and moral) Gentile.

After the War

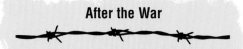

After the liberation, Schindler was welcomed by Jewish relief agencies and given money to start a new life in Argentina. But all his businesses failed, and in his last years Schindler returned to Europe and lived on handouts from his ever-grateful Jewish friends. After recognition in Israel for his rescue of so many Jews, he finally received a pension from the West German government in 1968. In the same year he received a papal knighthood. In 1967 he gave evidence against some of the Germans he had dealt with in the Cracow concentration camp.

When the work camp near Cracow was closed down and his workers were to be shipped to Auschwitz or to a labor camp, Schindler spent a small fortune bribing officials to let him take some of them to a relocated factory in Brinnlitz. Schindler got 1,100 of his workers to the safety of his new factory. At one stage the women were redirected to Auschwitz, and Schindler went there after them, buying them back from the commandant. By this time the war was near its end, and wagonloads of dying Jews were being shunted across Poland and Germany, taking them away from the approaching Russian troops. Schindler heard about one such wagonload of dying men and arranged for them to be brought to his factory. Those still alive were put in a warm corner of the factory floor on some straw. None of them weighed more than 75 lbs. (34 kilos)—as much as a young child.

Schindler's factory never actually made a single useful shell. It had become a cover for the survival of the more than 1,100 Jews whom Schindler was protecting.

Above: The factory in Cracow where Schindler's Jews made enamelware for the German war effort.

Raoul Wallenberg

In March 1944 the Nazis occupied Hungary. Two months later the deportations of thousands of Jews to Auschwitz began, even as the Russian troops advanced into Hungary from the east. In July, under increasing international pressure, the deportations were stopped. A Swedish diplomat, Raoul Wallenberg arrived in Budapest with visas for Jews to go to Sweden. A descendant of Swedish Jews, Wallenberg took over a number of houses, which were given diplomatic immunity (that is, they took on the legal status of Swedish territory and could not be entered by Hungarians or Germans). As many Jews as could be given visas both for Palestine and Sweden were housed in them. For a few months the war focused on other areas, and Budapest's Jews were left in relative peace. Then in October of that year an order went out for all Hungary's Jews to be marched into Germany for work in munitions factories. Jews with foreign passports were to be exempted, and so Wallenberg and the Swiss consul Charles Lutz set about issuing foreign passports to as many Hungarian Jews as they could. There is a record of one passport having held as many as 957 names! By bribery, cheating, and by any official means that he could, Wallenberg issued passports and visas and even drove to catch up with one of the death marches to issue passports to men and women being marched into Germany. When Russian troops finally entered Budapest, 120,000 Jews had survived, 25,000 of them in safe houses set up by Wallenberg and other foreign officials. Wallenberg reported to the Russian authorities and was arrested as a spy. It is thought that he died in a Russian prison.

Below: Raoul Wallenberg was one of a few foreign officials who broke every rule to rescue Jews. Another of these men was the Japanese consul in Kaunas, Lithuania, who issued visas for hundreds of people to go to Japan.

Eichmann Tries to Save Himself

In Hungary, Adolf Eichmann, one of the architects of the Final Solution, was put in charge of the evacuation of the Jews. When he saw that the war was nearly over, Eichmann offered Great Britain 1 million Jews in exchange for 10,000 trucks, which would only be used against the Russian troops, not the Western Allies. The man who negotiated with him was Saly Mayer, a Swiss Jew. The British and Americans refused to allow anything to be paid to the Nazis, but Mayer kept up the negotiations for months, probably delaying the deportations.

Below: Adolph Eichmann awaits trial in Israel in 1961.

Jewish Efforts at Rescue

Many Jews, living in disguise or in hiding, tried rescue attempts. In Greece, which was invaded by Germany in 1941, the Jewish religious leader Rabbi Ilia Barzilai escaped from Athens to Thessaly. He actively encouraged local Jewish men not yet rounded up by the Nazis to join the resistance. He also worked with Greek resistance fighters to get 600 Jews out of Greece by boat to Turkey. Another Greek rabbi, Rabbi Pessah, arranged for 752 Jews in Volos to be hidden by local people. In Hungary a Jew named Otto Komoly got permission to set up orphanages for 5,000 Jewish children. Most of the children survived until liberation, but Komoly was shot by the SS just before the Russian troops entered the city.

Jewish partisan groups in hiding in the woods of eastern Europe made many efforts to rescue Jews from the cities. In the Nolibocka forest in Belarus, the Bielski Otriad's aim was to rescue as many Jews as possible. Once the settlement was established, groups were sent into the ghettos to lead people out. The Bielski group also killed anyone who killed or betrayed Jews in hiding, making most people think carefully before committing such an act. The Bielski Otriad accomplished the largest rescue of Jews by Jews in occupied Europe.

Right: A French Red Cross worker helps a German prisoner of war.

Below: Taken in 1946, this photograph shows Rabbi Schonfeld (see page 13) with some of the children he helped to escape from Poland. He mounted a rescue operation and helped hundreds of Jews survive the Holocaust.

Sabina Zlatin

Sabina Zlatin was a Polish-born Jewish nurse who worked with the French Red Cross for most of the war. At first she worked in Agde, a concentration camp for foreign Jews in occupied France. She and others arranged for the entire camp to be removed to a more healthy location in the Pyrenees. She got permission to take 100 children a month out of the camp and put them into quarantine before being adopted by Gentile families. In 1943 she took 17 Jewish children out of the camp and hid them in the mountains east of Lyon. The children were betrayed by an informer and taken to the death camps. Because she was away when the children were arrested, Zlatin survived. She rejoined the resistance, and was wounded in an attack on a prison, but she survived the war.

Giving Testimony

In recent years hundreds of people have come forward, finally able to tell people what happened to them in the death camps, transports and ghettos. But even while the terrible events of 1939 to 1945 were taking place, there were people who, although they could not fight, knew that it was important to make a record of what was occurring. One of these was Emanuel Ringelbaum, who began a diary of the Nazi murders as early as 1938. While he was in the Warsaw ghetto he kept records of events and endeavored to get information to the outside world. His notes were hidden in the ghetto and recovered after his death in 1944. Like many others, he might have left the ghetto and got away safely but he felt it was his obligation to stay till the last. He praised the courage of the people who tried to help the Jews and kept a record of events both inside and outside the ghetto.

Left: At Babi Yar, a ravine outside Kiev, in Ukraine, 33,000 Jews were massacred by the Nazis in three days in 1941. Pictured here are three survivors of the massacre visiting the memorial to this event.

Another set of records was found in the ashes of those cremated in Auschwitz. Salmen Gradowski was sent to Auschwitz in February 1943. There, he saw his family burned in the crematorium at Birkenau and was made one of the *Sonderkommandos*, dragging corpses to the crematoriums. He and others buried messages and records of events, as well as human teeth, in the ashes so that after the war evidence of some of the deaths would remain. Gradowski went to the gas chamber in the autumn of 1944.

Above: This pond at Auschwitz contains the ashes of untold numbers of Jewish victims.

Salmen Gradowski

A letter, found in the ashes with the notes, reads:
Dear finder, search everywhere, in every inch of soil. Tens of documents are buried under it, mine and those of other persons, which will throw light on everything that was happening here. Great quantities of teeth are also buried here. It was we, the kommando workers, who expressly have strewn them all over the terrain, as many as we could, so that the world should find material traces of the millions of murdered people. We ourselves have lost hope of being able to live to see the moment of liberation.

(From Martin Gilbert, *The Holocaust:The Jewish Tragedy*, quoted from Jadwiga Bezwinska and Danuta Czech (eds), *Amidst a Nightmare of Crime*)

ARMED RESISTANCE

Fighting in the Ghettos

MOST OF the ghetto uprisings came late in the war. Many were tiny, with a only a few shots fired and a couple of Germans injured. In some cases, none of the Jews who witnessed them survived to tell the story. Unlike Gentile resistance groups, who fought for victory, Jewish resistance was carried out by those with no hope at all for the future.

On the night of September 23, 1942, in the town of Tuczyn, Poland—home to 3,000 Jews—rebellion broke out. The Jews had been ordered to assemble at the ghetto gates the next morning. Knowing that the order meant certain death, they began to destroy the ghetto, burning anything that might be of use to the Germans. German and Ukrainian troops began to fire into the ghetto. In the confusion, about 2,000 Jews escaped into the surrounding woods. Many were later rounded up and shot or surrendered to the police.

Below: In March 1942 nearly 12,000 Jews from the ghetto at Lublin, in Poland, were deported to Belzec extermination camp.

A Plea from a Resistance Fighter.

Many ghetto Jews were reluctant to rebel, hoping that they might sit out the war and thus be saved. This speech was made by one resistance leader in Vilnius after hundreds of people from the Vilnius ghetto had been taken to Ponar and shot:

No one returned of those who marched through the gates of the ghetto. All the roads of the Gestapo lead to Ponar. And Ponar means death. Those who waver, put aside all illusion. Your children, your wives, and husbands are no more. Ponar is no concentration camp. All were shot dead there. Hitler conspires to kill all the Jews of Europe, and the Jews of Lithuania have been picked at the first line. Let us not be led as sheep to the slaughter.

Brethren! Better fall as free fighters than to live at the mercy of murderers. Rise up! Rise up until your last breath.

(Quoted in Ruby Rohrlich (ed), *Resisting the Holocaust*)

The next month in the tiny ghetto of Marcinkonis, near Grodno, in Belarus, 370 Jews were assembled for deportation. The *Judenrat* leaders suddenly called out to the assembled group to flee for their lives. Barehanded, they attacked the Nazis. Although 105 died in the attack, the rest escaped into the woods.

In January 1943, several members of the underground movement in Czestochowa in Poland were caught up in an unexpected deportation. One of them, Mendel Fiszlewicz, attacked and wounded the German commander. He was quickly killed. As a reprisal, 25 men were shot, and 300 women and children were taken from the ghetto and sent to Treblinka death camp.

When the ghetto of Brody was emptied in May 1943, enough ordinary Jewish people resisted the deportations to kill several Ukrainians and Germans. They had bought weapons from the Italians guarding the ghetto. The sides of the cattle trucks used as vehicles for transport were beaten down by those inside, and hundreds of people jumped from them either to fall under the wheels, be shot down by the guards, or flee into the surrounding countryside.

Above: The ghetto in Cracow was liquidated in March 1943. The previous December a tiny number of Jewish resistance fighters had attacked a café used by SS officers. Most were hunted down and killed.

The Vilnius Ghetto

In Vilnius, Lithuania, the situation was complex. Although Vilnius was surrounded by forests, partisan groups frequently approached the ghetto to offer rescue, the resistance movement in Vilnius chose to remain in the ghetto as the protectors of the people. Ironically the people saw them as their greatest danger. The movement tried repeatedly to rouse the general population to rebellion, but they were hated and accused of bringing danger to the inhabitants. When the Nazis learned the name of the leader of the underground movement, Yitzhak Wittenberg, they demanded that he be surrendered to them. The *Judenrat* gave him up, but other members of the underground fought his captors and rescued him. He hid in the ghetto, and terrible reprisals were threatened if he did not surrender. Wittenberg surrendered in order to stop the reprisals. He was tortured and committed suicide.

But now that the Nazis were aware of the strength of the underground in Vilnius, they determined to liquidate the ghetto. Still rejected by the general population, the underground fled

Below: The Jewish Councils were often chosen by the Nazis and had to comply with their wishes. These young men and women were the staff of the Jewish Council in the Kielce ghetto in Poland.

Chaim Lazar

Chaim Lazar, a member of the underground in Vilnius, argued that the only hope for the ghetto dwellers was an armed rebellion. Like other members of the resistance in the Vilnius ghetto, he felt very bitter about the way that the other ghetto Jews had rejected the resistance's pleas for an insurrection. In his 1985 book about the ghetto, he wrote:

In the death cars, on the journey from which none returned, they would later recall how they attacked us. They would remember the stones they threw at us and the clubs they hit us with. They would recall the human sacrifice who offered himself in vain, and the blind stupidity of the fraternal war in the presence of the common enemy, and perhaps they would find atonement for their sins.

(From Chaim Lazar, *Destruction and Resistance*, quoted in Ruby Rohrlich (ed.) *Resisting the Holocaust*)

into the forests. In September 1943 the ghetto was emptied, its 20,000 occupants taken to the death camps. The underground, now a partisan group in the woods, carried out attacks on German troop movements and became an important part of the partisan movement. But it had not been able to save its own community.

Above: This photo shows Vilnius today, as the capital of the independent nation of Lithuania.

The Warsaw Ghetto Uprising

The Warsaw ghetto uprising was the most significant and well documented of the many desperate attempts at resistance made by Jews in eastern Europe. When the Warsaw ghetto was first established, all those living in it hoped that the war would end soon and they would be liberated. Among them were tiny political groups and resistance groups, whose members were very young and determined not to go "like lambs to the slaughter." It was many months before starvation and deportations to the death camps made the situation in the ghetto truly desperate. At this point, the underground movements were able to organize themselves. Like the underground movements in other cities, the people knew they would be fighting a hopeless war that would end in their deaths.

Although the ghetto was officially sealed, there were many ways of contacting the outside. Gradually, the underground persuaded the Polish resistance to supply them with a few meager handguns and grenades. They bought other weapons on the black market in Warsaw.

Below: An old Jewish man collapses on the streets of Warsaw.

An Eyewitness Account

Though the unit was destroyed, the battle on Niska Street encouraged us. For the first time since the occupation we saw Germans clinging to the walls, crawling on the ground, running for cover, hesitating before making a step for fear of being hit by a Jewish bullet. The cries of the wounded caused us joy and increased our thirst for battle.

(Tuvia Borzykowski, *Between Tumbling Walls*, quoted in Martin Gilbert, *The Holocaust: The Jewish Tragedy*)

The first act of open resistance came in January 1943, when many Jews, including armed resistance fighters, were being deported to the Treblinka death camp. Suddenly, the resistance fighters, led by a man named Mordechai Anielewicz, began to throw grenades, killing some of the Germans. Most of the people were killed immediately, but others barricaded themselves inside a building. The Germans brought in reinforcements and set the building on fire. Inside, those with guns continued to fire on the Germans until they were killed by German fire. A massive search of the ghetto ensued, with hundreds of people randomly killed. The resistance took to the rooftops, killing Germans and taking their weapons. The fighting continued for two more days, and 12 Germans were killed. Strangely, considering their enormous superiority, the Germans withdrew from the ghetto. If they had known that the resistance fighters had only a few guns and little ammunition left, they would surely have continued until the last death, preventing the major rebellion that occurred the following April.

Above: As the houses in the Warsaw ghetto began to burn, people jumped to avoid the flames but were shot down in the process.

Warsaw Ghetto—the Final Battle

The following April word spread around the Warsaw ghetto that it was about to be cleared and its inhabitants sent to the death and slave labor camps. The resistance movement was ready for this. Hundreds of bunkers had been built for the unarmed in the hope that in the chaos they could escape through the sewers into the city. The Polish resistance had been impressed by the way that ordinary Jews had carried themselves during the previous battle and decided to give the Jews more weapons. The Jews were armed with two submachine guns, 17 rifles, about 500 pistols, and thousands of homemade grenades and gasoline bombs. They were outnumbered two to one by the Germans and outgunned by tanks and hundreds of machine guns. Even so, the Germans were driven out of the ghetto again on the first day; 12 were killed, and their weapons were taken away. In the following days the Germans fired mortar bombs and high-caliber machine guns into the ghetto. Buildings started to burn.

Left: From outside the ghetto walls, automatic weapons were used to kill as many people as possible.

Left: German troops patrol the defeated and burning Warsaw ghetto.

The battle lasted from April 19 to May 16. Hundreds died and thousands were transported, many of them to Treblinka and Majdanek labor camps, where they continued to resist and were killed. An estimated several thousand escaped into the city. People continued to hide out in bunkers in the ghetto until the following September, when the ghetto was razed.

Nina Boniwna

Fourteen years old when she was caught up in the ghetto uprising in Warsaw, Nina narrowly escaped with her life. Her family was hiding in some carts when they were discovered. Her mother was sent to be deported, her brother was sent to a smaller ghetto, and Nina was lined up against a wall to be shot:

I stood against the wall. I felt no fear at all. Everyone was flashing before my eyes, and I realized that I would never see anybody ever again.

When the man in front of me fell, I felt afraid. They shot him twice and in the end

they had to finish him off with a bayonet. I was not afraid of such suffering so much as aware of the fact that none of my loved ones were with me. At the last moment a woman friend of ours shoved me onto the cart and pinned the necessary number on me, fooling the guard with her quick and unexpected action.

Later Nina escaped from the ghetto into Warsaw, where she survived until liberation.

(Quoted in Maria Hochberg-Mariańska and Noe Grüss, *The Children Accuse*)

Bialystok

By summer 1943 most of the ghettos of eastern Europe had been emptied and their inhabitants sent to extermination centers or to work camps to die a slower death. The ghettos that remained— Lodz, Vilnius, Bialystok, Czestochowa—were the largest. The survivors there were those who could prove that they were useful workers in the local slave factories. The Warsaw ghetto uprising had been a great moral victory, but it had convinced the Germans that as the Jews became more desperate and were no longer fooled by the stories of resettlement in the east, they were becoming a danger.

In Bialystok an underground movement had also developed. Unlike in other ghettos, the underground was on good terms with the *Judenrat* and accepted the leader's view that they should not do anything to provoke an attack on the ghetto. They agreed that they should wait until deportation was imminent before trying to fight back. When the day came in August 1943, the underground was not ready. They had few weapons, their plan to burn down the factories failed, and the general population went to the transports

Below: The Polish Home Army, an underground movement, celebrates mass. At the end of the war hundreds of Jewish survivors died at the hands of Polish anti-Semites.

Bertha Sokolskaya

One of the last people to be deported from Bialystok was Bertha Sokolskaya. She was confined with 40 other people in a freight car. While she was in it she heard that some people from another car had forced a way out and escaped. Weak from heat and thirst, the women in her car decided it would be better to die:

There was amongst us a doctor from Lodz, Chanoleskaya, who had a razor and she began slashing our wrists. We were beside ourselves, pushing and shoving and stretching out our hands. She cut one of my wrists and a fountain of blood burst out and I fell... next morning the Germans opened the door. I was still alive.

(Quoted in Martin Gilbert, *The Holocaust: The Jewish Tragedy*)

Above: In the dead of winter Jews were crowded into open freight cars destined for the slave labor camps in Germany.

offering no resistance at all. A gun battle took place in one section of the ghetto, as the young militants set fire to whatever buildings they could, in the hope that some people would escape into the woods. But none did. The resisters held out as long as they could against tanks and heavy weaponry, but eventually they were defeated. A tiny number got away into the woods.

Jewish Partisan Groups

In the ghettos people chose to fight street battles against their murderers. Others chose to escape and join partisan groups. These were guerrilla movements, supporting the ideals of their own country, and in many cases they were nearly as anti-Semitic as the Germans. Later in the war, the Soviet Union sent its own partisan groups into the woods, often dropping them by parachute.

Tuvia Bielski's group, operating in the woods of Belarus, has already been mentioned in its efforts to rescue and hide Jews. In addition it was an active fighting unit, attacking German vehicles and the families of German policemen. One unit dedicated itself entirely to attacking German troops, cutting telegraph wires, and fighting search parties that came into the woods.

In the Parczew forest in Poland many Jews were hiding among the trees. Many of them were dying of hunger and many had been caught in manhunts. In late 1942 a Jew named Yekhiel Grynspan escaped into the forest. Aged 24, he quickly found others who could fight. They obtained weapons from local Poles and spent the next two years, until Soviet troops infiltrated the woods and took command, attacking German and Ukrainian police posts and even setting fire to the German police headquarters in Parczew town.

In May 1942, Moyshe Gildeman established a Jewish partisan group in Volhynia, sabotaging train lines and storage depots. In

Left: Yekhiel Grynspan, stands fourth from the left in this picture, with other Jewish partisans. They had escaped from the trains taking Jews to Sobibor extermination camp. The partisans protected Jews in the Parczew forest in Poland.

January 1943 they were accepted into the Soviet partisan army as a special Jewish unit. Another Jewish group led by Haim Henry Rozenson joined the same group. Another group in Belarus, led by Abba Kovner, who had escaped with other underground members from the Vilnius ghetto, destroyed two bridges and two train locomotives, as well as many telegraph poles. Many more small fighting units perished in battles with the German troops.

Left: The Vilnius partisans return to the ghetto after liberation in July 1944. Vitka Kempner is at the far right and Abba Kovner is fourth from the right. They married after the war.

Vitka Kempner

A resident of the Vilnius ghetto, in 1943, Kempner blew up a German military train and escaped back to the ghetto. Two months later she blew up a transformer inside Vilnius, then smuggled out several dozen prisoners in the nearby labor camp. Later in the war she joined a partisan group and burned down a turpentine factory in the town of Olkiniki. A survivor, Hava Shurek, describes seeing Vitka after she had blown up the train:

There was a strength in her eyes which gave them an unusual brightness.... When she was asked what she had thought during the long night, she answered: "How to do the job without falling into their hands..." (The Germans) did not suspect the Jews, for they were sure that the Jews were already defeated and would not raise their heads. Such a deed could only be done by free men.

(Quoted in Martin Gilbert, The Nazi Holocaust: The Jewish Tragedy)

Armed Resistance and Escape Attempts in the Camps

By the time most people arrived in the death camps or the work camps, they had endured months of starvation, the loss of their families, illness, and the horror of being transported in railroad cars. The fact that any rebellions at all took place in these camps is remarkable. The attacks rarely resulted in anything more than the deaths of the people who made them.

In 1942, when the labor camp at Kruszyna was being liquidated, the Jews attacked their guards with knives and fists. Six died but four escaped. On the way to the transports more resistance resulted in the deaths of those who refused to board the cattle cars. Three weeks later the labor camp near Minsk in Belarus was emptied and again the inmates resisted, barricading themselves inside a building, which was burned to the ground with 400 people inside. In August 1943, at Babi Yar, in the suburbs of Kiev, 400 Jews and Soviet POWs were forced to open mass graves and burn the corpses. (The Germans had begun to fear that the war might end in defeat for them and that there would be retribution for their treatment of the Jews. All over German-occupied eastern

Below: In the ghettos, disease and malnutrition killed many people.

Sobibor

One of the more successful armed breakouts took place at Sobibor in 1943. There were 600 Jews in the labor camp, many of them teenagers. Led by a Jewish Red Army POW, they planned a breakout. Girls working in the staff quarters stole weapons and knives, and hatchets were made. Warm clothing was hidden. On October 13, the Jews were ready. Weapons were distributed and the order was given. Nine SS men and two Ukrainians were killed and 300 people escaped into the woods. The rest were killed. About 10 of those who escaped survived the war.

Left: This memorial was erected to the victims of the Babi Yar massacre.

Europe, records and corpses were being destroyed.) Jews worked in inhuman conditions, wearing shackles. Executions took place at random. As they hauled the rotting corpses out of the mass graves, the Jews searched them for keys, hoping that they might find one to fit the bunker that they were locked up in each night. Miraculously, such a key was found, and 325 Jews and POWs escaped. Then, 311 were shot down as they ran, but 14 escaped, 10 of them surviving the war.

Treblinka

At Treblinka death camp there were several planned attempts at armed breakouts. In 1943 a Jewish doctor, Julian Chorazycki, found a Ukrainian guard who was willing to supply weapons for cash. Several weapons thereby came into Jewish hands. But in April of that year Chorazycki was discovered and took poison, having first wounded the SS officer who exposed him. In June, 40 hand grenades were smuggled into the camp, but they proved to be defective. In August the inmates broke into the camp arsenal (weapon store-room) and stole 40 guns and some grenades. At the same time, the huts were sprayed with gasoline. At a given signal, the huts were torched and the rebellion began. Sixteen guards were killed, and 150 people escaped. The rest of the 700 camp inmates were killed. The camp was evacuated that year, and the remaining prisoners were given the task of destroying the evidence. Thirteen of them were working outside the fence when one, Seweryn Klajnman, aged 18, killed the guard, put on his uniform, and marched the others away from the camp. All 13 escaped.

Right: A reconstruction at Auschwitz of the crematorium ovens. The originals were destroyed immediately after liberation.

Below: Treblinka death camp as it looks today.

Revolt at Auschwitz-Birkenau

In 1943 at Birkenau, a group of women destined for the gas chambers rebelled after one, whose surname was Horowitz, grabbed a gun and shot two guards. Inspired by her action, the women attacked the guards, tearing off the nose of one and scalping another. All the women were shot. One of the guards that Horowitz had shot was well known for strangling Jews with his bare hands. He died of his wounds. The next year a revolt took place among the 500 Sonderkommandos, all Greek Jews who had watched their families killed. Some girls working in the munitions factory stole explosives for them. At a roll call, one of the Sonderkommandos attacked the guards with his bare hands, ran to crematorium IV, and packed the explosives into it. The crematorium exploded. When other groups saw the crematorium ablaze, they used the chaos to cut the fence and run. Most were cut down by machine-gun fire, but 12 escaped and remained at large for a few hours before being found and shot. The girls who had stolen the explosives were discovered and tortured before execution. All 600 Sonderkommandos were executed in the wake of the rebellion—except for three doctors, one of whom, Miklos Nyiszli, survived to tell the story. Of all the violent rebellions in the camps, this was the only one that actually hindered the Nazi effort to kill Jews by putting one of the crematoriums out of action.

Mala and Edek

Caught up in the Nazi trap when Germany invaded Belgium, Mala Zimetbaum, age 20, found herself in Auschwitz working as a runner taking messages from one part of the vast camp complex to another. This was a very useful job, and Mala often found out information that she was able to pass on to prisoners to help them. She was a very popular person, and everyone in the camp was pleased when she and her lover, Edek Galiski, escaped, disguised as an SS officer and a prisoner. Edek had stolen the uniform and Mala had stolen the pass.

Various stories have been told about how they were recaptured, but they were at large for several weeks before they were brought back to the camp. Mala was tortured and taken to be hanged in front of the assembled women of Auschwitz. Before they could kill her, she cut her wrists and was hauled off to the crematorium. Edek similarly refused to be murdered by throwing himself into the noose and kicking loose the stool he was standing on, before the hanging could be done officially. Many Auschwitz survivors tell this story about two people's escape and re-arrest. It stands out as a triumph of young lovers against the

Left: The barbed wire fences are a reminder of the horrors of Auschwitz and its satellite camps.

Above: Older women and children were often immediately selected to go to the gas chambers. These people were probably dead within hours of this picture being taken.

vast Nazi machine. Even though they died, they had still had a few weeks together on the outside, and they took their own lives rather than allowing the Nazis to murder them. The significance of their escape can be seen in the fact that the Germans didn't kill them on the spot, a fate suffered by countless thousands of runaway Jews—but brought them back to the camp to show the other prisoners that there was no escape.

Reactions to the Escape

Fania Fenelon, a member of the Auschwitz orchestra, recalls how she felt when Mala and Edek escaped:

We were insanely gleeful. Our reasoning was over-simple but heartening: Since they're out, we'll be freed. We were beside ourselves.... We could already see Mala and Edek returning at the head of millions of soldiers, who would enter the camp and put out the SS men's eyes, bayonet them in the stomach. We were drunk with images of gory revenge. For the first time since our internment we lived and breathed hope.... There were vicious searches throughout the camps, interrogations in the SS building, accomplices were sought. But everyone claimed ignorance and it was true.

(From Fania Fenelon, *Playing for Time*, quoted in Otto Friedrich, *The Kingdom of Auschwitz*)

LIKE LAMBS TO THE SLAUGHTER?

U NTHINKING PEOPLE often ask why so many Jewish people went to their deaths without a struggle, "like lambs to the slaughter." The stories here, and the many hundreds of others, show that Jews and others did fight to save Jewish lives. During the war thousands of people—Soviet POWs, strong young men, Communists, homosexuals and Gypsies—also tragically went to their deaths in the camps. Because the Nazis were so powerful, resistance required a superhuman effort, making it all the more remarkable that anyone was able to fight back.

By the time that the liquidation of the ghettos began, most young people had been taken to work camps, and a large proportion of those that remained were the elderly, sick, or children. They were hardly the most likely people to take up arms, even if they could.

Those who did take up arms did so under the most difficult circumstances. Jewish underground groups had little support from Polish or Russian partisans, no assistance from the Western Allied forces, no weapons except those that they could steal or make themselves, and no strength on a starvation diet and

Left: German children playing happily in the years before the Holocaust. These may well have been the adults who turned their backs while their Jewish neighbors went to the ghettos and death camps.

Left: This inmate of Bergen-Belsen concentration camp was a Hungarian Jew sent to Belsen as a political prisoner. Hunger, inhuman working conditions, and brutal treatment took their toll on his health.

unhealthy living conditions. They also faced the violent opposition of the ghetto Jews.

Worse still perhaps was the inability to overcome the belief that nothing as insane as the Holocaust could possibly be happening in a modern, civilized society. The Jews in the ghettos, where resistance should have been the greatest, had no contact with the outside world. They had no evidence, except for some rumors that the mass murders were taking place, and they were daily persuaded by the Nazis that all would be well if they would just cooperate. After years of anti-Semitic abuse, of being told that they were less than human, a disease, a threat to society, they had been made to feel isolated, helpless, and ashamed. Such feelings could often prove to be stronger than the anger and injustice felt at what was happening to them.

The Survivors

Who were the survivors?

A larger proportion of people who took action to save themselves survived than those who were unable to act. Because emigration and hiding were expensive and only available to a limited number of people, a relatively small number of people were able to take these actions. On the other hand, in the early days of Hitler's rise to power, many wealthy people chose to stay rather than abandon everything that they had in Germany.

Below: Few of the millions who died had their ashes treated this carefully. This is an official SS photograph from Theresienstadt, a ghetto that the Germans attempted to turn into a model settlement and allowed the Red Cross to visit.

• Because of the selection process at the camps, few children under the age of 10, elderly people, people with disabilities, or women with small children survived the war.
• Some wealthy or prominent Jews were sent to Theresienstadt, a model camp where life, although harsh, was not deadly. Many survived.
• Some Hungarian Jews survived because German forces occupied Hungary late in the war, and the killing machine just didn't have time to get to them. Still, 200,000 of Hungary's 500,000 Jews were killed.

Jewish Resignation

Jan Karski, a member of the Polish Home Army, the underground resistance movement that operated in Poland during the war, recalls what one Jew told him:

After the war Poland will be resurrected. Your cities will be rebuilt and your wounds will slowly heal. From this ocean of tears, pain, rage and humiliation your country will emerge again but the Polish Jews will no longer exist. We will be dead. Hitler will lose the war against the human, the just and the good, but he will win the war against the Polish Jews. No, it will not be a victory; the Jewish people will be murdered.

(From Jan Karski, *Story of a Secret State*, quoted in Michael Marrus, *The Holocaust in History*)

A Buried Message from One of the Sonderkommandos

And there a girl of five stood and undressed her brother who was one year old. One from the kommando came to take off the boy's clothes. The girl shouted loudly "Be gone, you Jewish murderer! Don't lay your hands, dripping with Jewish blood, upon my lovely brother! I am his good mummy, he will die in my arms together with me." A boy of seven or eight stood beside her and spoke thus, "Why, you are a Jew and you lead such dear children to the gas chamber—only in order to live? Is your life among the band of murderers really dearer to you than the lives of so many Jewish victims?"

(Quoted in Martin Gilbert, *The Holocaust: The Jewish Tragedy*)

• Danish and Norwegian Jews survived because of public attempts to help them.
• Finnish and Italian Jews survived because their governments refused to give them up.
• Others in the death camps survived because their strength of will, religious beliefs, or sense of survival made it possible.
• For others the expression that one survivor used, "tainted luck," is the only reason that they survived. They just happened not to die.

In general the massive killing machine invented by the Nazis for ridding Europe of people they considered unworthy of life was very efficient. Those who survived their onslaught did so because of minor inefficiencies of the system, as well as through enormous courage and resourcefulness.

Left: In modern Warsaw the ghetto area is now a series of housing projects, but there are many memorials (in Polish and English, not Hebrew or Yiddish) marking key spots in the defense of the ghetto.

TIMELINE

1939
September *Einsatzgruppen* begin mass exterminations in Poland.

December Labor camps set up throughout Poland. All Jewish males required for forced labor.

1940
May Lodz ghetto sealed off.

October Deportations to the Warsaw ghetto begin.

October Foreign Jews interned in Vichy France.

1941
February Deportations of Dutch Jews to German concentration camps.

June Invasion of Soviet Union. *Einsatzgruppen* massacres extend to Baltic states and western Ukraine.

September Construction of Birkenau death camp begins.

December Gas vans begin operation at Chelmno.

1942
January Resistance movement begins to organize itself in Vilnius.

March First transports of Polish Jews to the death camps.

July Mass deportations of Dutch Jews to Auschwitz.

July Deportations begin in Warsaw.

October Deportations of Jews from Norway. Many escape.

November Deportations begin in the Bialystok region of Poland.

November German Gypsies deported to Auschwitz.

1943
March Deportations of Greek Jews to Auschwitz.

March Cracow ghetto closed. Schindler's Jews move into his factory site.

April–May Warsaw ghetto uprising.

May Schmuel Zygielbojm commits suicide in London.

June Lvov ghetto liquidated.

August Attempted breakout from Treblinka.

August Bialystok ghetto cleared. Attempted revolt put down.

September Danish Jews ferried to safety in Sweden.

September Vilnius ghetto liquidated.

October Breakout from Sobibor.

October Deportations of Italian Jews to Auschwitz.

1944
May Deportations of Hungarian Jews begin.

July Death marches begin. Majdanek death camp liberated by Red Army.

August Lodz ghetto liquidated.

October Inmates blow up one of the crematoriums at Auschwitz.

November Wallenberg intercedes on behalf of Hungarian Jews.

November Gas chambers destroyed at Auschwitz by the Nazis.

1945
January Death marches out of Poland into Germany.

January Auschwitz liberated.

May Germany surrenders. Jews continue to die in German concentration camps, now all liberated.

RESOURCES

FURTHER READING AND SOURCES

Bauer, Yehuda. *History of the Holocaust*. Danbury, CT: Franklin Watts, 1992.

Dawidowicz, Lucy. *The War Against the Jews*. New York: Penguin, 1990.

Frank, Anne. *The Diary of Anne Frank*. New York: Bantam, 1993.

Friedlander, Saul. *Nazi Germany and the Jews: The Years of Persecution 1933-1939*. New York: HarperCollins, 1998.

Gilbert, Martin. *The Holocaust*. New York: Henry Holt, 1987.

Grant, R. G. *The Holocaust: New Perspectives*. New York: Raintree Steck-Vaughn, 1998.

Gutman, Israel. *Resistance: The Warsaw Ghetto Uprising*. New York: Houghton-Mifflin, 1997.

Hilberg, Raul. *The Destruction of the European Jews*. Holmes and Meier, 1985.

Keneally, Thomas. *Schindler's List*. Touchstone, 1993.

Laquer, Walter (ed). *The Holocaust Encyclopedia*. New Haven, CT: Yale University Press, 2001.

Levi, Primo. *Survival in Auschwitz*. New York: Simon and Schuster, 1996.

Rohrlich, Ruby (ed.) *Resisting the Holocaust*. New York: Berg, 1998.

Wiesel, Elie. *Night*. New York: Bantam, 1982.

INTERNET SITES

Shoah Visual History Foundation
www.vhf.org
Photographs and stories by survivors.

United States Holocaust Memorial Museum
www.ushmn.org
Pictorial history of the Holocaust

Yad Veshem
www.yad-vashem.org
Official website for the Holocaust Martyrs' and Heroes' Remembrance Authority

FILMS

The following movies are available for rent as videos or DVDs:

Schindler's List. Directed by Steven Spielberg from the book by Thomas Keneally, this is the story of a German factory owner who saved more than 1,000 Jews.

Shoah. Directed by Claude Lanzmann, this is a nine-hour documentary consisting entirely of interviews with survivors of and participants in the Holocaust.

Life is Beautiful. Directed by and starring Roberto Benigni, this controversial, Academy Award-winning film tells the fictional tale of an Italian Jewish father who creates a kind of make-believe contest out of the Nazi occupation in order to shelter his son from the horrors of the Holocaust.

PLACES TO VISIT

United States Holocaust Memorial Museum
100 Raoul Wallenberg Place SW
Washington, D.C. 20024
Phone: (202) 488-0400
Website: www.ushm.org
Library: library@ushm.org
(202) 479-9717

GLOSSARY

anti-Semitism prejudice against Jewish people.

Aryan in Nazi ideology, a white-skinned northern European, not of Jewish descent.

atonement a way of seeking forgiveness for a sin.

Auschwitz–Birkenau the major killing center in the Nazi empire. It extended over several miles and included satellite work camps besides the three main camps. Auschwitz I, the original work camp; Birkenau, the extermination camp; and Monowitz, the industrial center.

Babi Yar a ravine on the outskirts of Kiev in the Ukraine, where approximately 33,000 Jews were murdered by the *Einsatzgruppen.*

Belarus a small country between Poland and Russia in Europe.

Baumgruppe a Jewish resistance group that operated in Berlin until 1942.

communism the theory that all property should be state-owned and that each person should be paid according to his or her needs.

concentration camps large-scale prison and work camps where prisoners were often worked to death but not in the systematic manner of the death camps.

consuls officials who work for their country in a foreign city to protect their fellow citizens in that country.

cyanide of potassium a poison.

Dachau a concentration camp in Germany; one of the first to be established.

dehumanize to deprive people of basic human rights so that they feel inferior and weakened.

death camps centers where Jews, Gypsies, and homosexuals were sent to be murdered. The chief death camps were all in Poland: Auschwitz-Birkenau, Belzec, Chelmno, Majdanek, Sobibor, and Treblinka.

death marches the forced evacuation of camp inmates in the final stages of the war.

Einsatzgruppen special German mobile units responsible for large-scale massacres of Poles, Russian Jews, Communists and intellectuals.

extermination the destruction of a living thing.

Final Solution the Nazi term for the extermination of European Jews.

Fascist originally the name of an extreme right-wing nationalist group established in Italy in the 1920s, the term is now applied to all political parties of a nationalist, racist, and extreme right-wing nature.

Gentiles non-Jews.

ghettos a section of a city where Jews were forced to live.

Hanukkah the Jewish festival of light, commemorating the purification of the temple in 165 B.C..

insurrection an uprising or armed rebellion against authority.

Judenrat "Jewish Council," the representative body established by the Nazis in the ghettos. They administered Nazi decrees.

kapos Nazi-appointed overseers in the camps, usually German criminals rather than Jews or Poles.

labor camp a camp dedicated to the German war effort, using Jews, POWs, and other citizens of occupied states.

liquidate to kill something.

Lvov a town in Lithuania with a large ghetto population.

Mischling a person of mixed Jewish ancestry, some of whom were allowed to stay in Germany.

Nazi Party (Nationalsozialistische Deutsche Arbeiterpartei) in English "National Socialist German Workers' Party". Led by Hitler, the Nazi Party governed Germany between 1933 and 1945.

partisans underground freedom fighters who fought the Nazis.

pogrom mass murder of people by a mob of their fellow citizens. The term usually applies to the attacks on Jews.

resistance (French) an organization that is fighting secretly within an occupied country for liberation (freedom).

Shoah Hebrew for Holocaust.

Sonderkommando a special squad whose job it was to lead people to the gas chambers and then dispose of the bodies.

Theresienstadt a "model" concentration camp near Prague created in November 1941 and used to calm Western suspicions about the fate of the Jews.

Untermenschen in Nazi ideology, subhumans, or people of inferior race.

Vichy France a German-controlled French government set up in southern France after the German conquest.

INDEX